# Mishnah
## and the
# Words
of
# Jesus

Dr. Roy B. Blizzard is president of Bible Scholars, Inc., an Austin-based corporation dedicated to biblical research and education. He is the author of *The Bible Sex and You, Tithing Giving and Prosperity, The Mountain of the Lord, Let Judah go up first: A study in praise, prayer, and worship*, and coauthor of *Understanding the Difficult Words of Jesus: New Insights From a Hebrew Perspective*. Visit the Bible Scholars website at www.biblescholars.org.

# Mishnah

## and the

# Words

## of

# Jesus

Roy B. Blizzard

Bible Scholars, Inc.
Austin, Texas

Cover design: Sue Schoenfeld

P.O. Box 204073
Austin, Texas 78720
www.biblescholars.org

Printed in the United States of America

# CONTENTS

# FOREWORD

After finishing this manuscript on the *Mishnah* and the words of Jesus, it occurred to me that probably many people know little or nothing about the *Mishnah* or the way the Rabbis taught in the time of Jesus. What were they teaching? What were their methods of teaching? It is safe to say that the focus of all rabbinic teaching was the law. For the rabbis, the law consisted not only of the written but of the oral as well. The "Written Law" was the *Torah* or the five books of Moses – *Genesis, Exodus, Leviticus, Numbers*, and *Deuteronomy* – that God gave Israel at Sinai. In additional to this written revelation, Moses had also received, according to the rabbis, additional spoken laws. The rabbis designated these as the "Oral Law", *torah sheh b'al peh*, as distinguished from the "Written Law", *torah sheh-bichtav*. And they considered these to be as inspired and as binding as the Written Law. The opening of *Avot*, a tractate or chapter in the *Mishnah*, records:

Moses received the Torah from Sinai, and transmitted it to Joshua, and Joshua to the elders, and the elders to the prophets, and the prophets transmitted it to the men of the Great Assembly (1:1).

*"Torah"* here refers specifically to the Oral Law, as distinguished from the Written. And following 1:1 is a list of three sayings attributed to the men of the Great Assembly:

1. Be slow in rendering legal decisions (verdicts),
2. Educate many students,
3. Erect a protective fence around the Law.

Following these sayings is a saying of Simon the Just, one of the last survivors of the Great Assembly. Then comes a saying of Antigonus of Socho that he received from Simon the Just. From this saying onward until the end of *Avot* are listed the sayings of a string of rabbis, each of whom received his saying from his immediate predecessor.

The rabbis viewed the Oral Law as beginning with Moses and being passed, saying by saying and generation by generation. The Oral had been given to Moses at Sinai along with the Written Law and so has coexisted with it ever since.

Additional laws not found in the Written Law appear in the Oral Law as, "laws given to Moses at Sinai." The rest of the Oral Law is implied in the Written Law and can be deduced from it by principles of interpretation developed by rabbis during the time of Jesus. That those rabbis viewed both the Written Law and the Oral Law as having been given at Sinai is verified by an anecdote about a contemporary of Jesus, the famous Rabbi Shammai (50 BCE-30 CE):

> It is related that a certain man stood before Shammai and said, 'Rabbi, how many Torahs do you have?' The rabbi replied, 'Two – one written and one oral' (*Avot d'Rabbi Natan*) (*Shabbat* 31a).

A second anecdote, at a later time and involving another rabbi, attests to the same.

> The Roman governor Quietus asked Rabban Gamaliel II about the number of *Torahs*. He replied (ca 117 CE) as Shammai: 'two – one written and one oral.'

For a rabbi in the time of Jesus, the Oral Law included much more than just those laws spoken by God to Moses at Sinai. It included, more widely, all the traditional readings of Scripture and all the ethical maxims and rulings passed down by former rabbis, even those of his own generation. Yet the rabbis did not consider all these to be new. Rather, as having already existed when the Law was given at Sinai. "Even that which a distinguished student was destined to teach in the presence of his teacher, the rabbis said, 'was already said to Moses on Sinai'" (*Jerusalem Talmud* 17a). The work of rabbis through the ages, then, was that of a mirror rather than that of a lamp. They did not say new things. Rather, they said old things in new ways – reflected them anew.

Because of a rabbinic aversion to transmitting oral material to writing, the entire body of Oral Law was not thus transmitted until the beginning of the 3rd century CE. The origin of this aversion is not known, but its force appears in a remark by Judah ben Nachmani: "What has been said orally one may not say in writing, and vice versa" (*Gittin* 60b). And a kindred remark, by Rabbi Yochanan, adds to this force – although by the time of Nachmani and Yochanan the Oral Law was already in the process of being transmitted to writing: "He who records oral laws is like him who burns the Torah; and whoever studies these collections has no reward" (*Temurah* 14b). However, in spite of this aversion, the Oral Law began to be transmitted to writing at the beginning of the 3rd century CE.

The first compilation of Oral Law into written form for public use was the *Mishnah*. It was compiled by Rabbi Yehudah ha-Nasi (ca 200 CE). Once he broke with tradition and published his work, similar compilations followed, incorporating materials he had not used. One such compilation is the *Tosephta* "supplement" or "addition." It is about four times larger than the *Mishnah*, is divided in the same manner, and contains the same kind of material. The *Tosephta* appeared early in the 5th century CE, roughly 200 years after the *Mishnah* of Rabbi Yehudah.

Both the *Mishnah* and the *Tosephta* contain readings, rulings, and maxims divided into six orders: *Zeraim*, "seeds"; *Moed*, "festivals"; *Nashim*, "women"; *Nezikin*, "damages"; *Kodashim*, "sacred things"; and *Tohorot*, "purity." These orders then subdivide into 63 books or tractates. Both compilations also contain detailed commentaries on the five books of the *Torah* – with exegeses of not merely chapters but, as well, of verses and even words within these chapters. These commentaries are *Mekhilta*, *Sifra*, and *Sifre*. *Mekhilta* (a measuring vessel) is a commentary on most of the *Book of Exodus*. *Sifra* (a book) is a commentary on the entire *Book of Leviticus.* And *Sifre* (books) contains rabbinic rulings and commentary on large portions of the *Book of Numbers* and *Book of Deuteronomy.*

But even these far-reaching works did not exhaust all of the oral traditions and Scriptural commentary extant when Rabbi Yehudah began compiling his *Mishnah.* Much additional Oral Law is to be found in the *Gemara*, a commentary on the *Mishnah.* The *Gemara*, together with the *Mishnah*, is known as the *Talmud.* There are two versions of the *Talmud*: one compiled by Jewish scholars in Babylon (the *Babylonian Talmud*) and one compiled by Jewish scholars in the Land of Israel (the *Jerusalem Talmud*).

*Talmud page*

Being the work of two different schools of scholars, the *Gemara* in one version of the *Talmud* differs markedly from that in the other. But the *Mishnah* in both is the *Mishnah* of Rabbi Yehudah. The *Babylonian Talmud* was completed ca 500 CE, the *Jerusalem Talmud* roughly a century earlier. It is a gigantic sea of rabbinic learning, consisting of 2,500,000 words spread over 5,894 folio pages roughly 10 1/2 x 14 inches in size. Although the Jerusalem Talmud is also a monumental work, it is 10 times smaller than the *Babylonian.*

The *Babylonian Talmud* is today the focus of Jewish religious education. And when the word *Talmud* appears alone, the reference is understood to be the *Babylonian* as opposed to the *Jerusalem Talmud.* The *Talmud* holds the position of highest esteem in Orthodox Judaism. To study it, to be illuminated by it, is the goal of every young orthodox Jewish man. In Jewish circles, sages or scholars of the *Talmud* are looked upon as the hero would be in the secular realm. Indeed, to the Orthodox, the *melumad* or Talmudic scholar is the real hero of their world.

# CHAPTER 1
# *TZEDAKAH* AND
# RIGHTEOUSNESS

In this book we will study comparisons between the words of Jesus and the words of rabbis prior to, contemporary with, and following Jesus, recorded for us in the *Mishnah, Order Nezikin, Tractate Avot,* or the *Chapters of the Fathers.*

In the teachings of Jesus, there is one underlying and overriding theme, a theme on which Jesus consistently dwells, a theme that serves as the foundation upon which biblical faith is built. If one looks at the *Bible* as a whole, if one includes additionally all Jewish literature that is extant, the Oral Law, the Written Law, the commentaries, and search for one, single, overriding theme that is the foundational theme of biblical faith, one would have to conclude that that foundational theme is summed up in the Hebrew word *tzedakah*, the word frequently translated into English as righteousness. *Tzedakah* is the outstanding, overriding, and yet simple, theme of Jesus.

I have been deeply concerned for some time because it appears that Christianity has little or no understanding of true biblical faith. It has lost the real focus of biblical faith. It seems the people of God simply do not understand what biblical faith is all about. What I am about to say, I am saying not to be offensive or irreverent, and I hope you will not be offended because it is not meant to offend.

I am concerned that in everything we see, everything we do, and everywhere we go today in Christianity, the focus is upon what? Jesus. It is all we hear. Jesus. Christianity has become an other-worldly religion to the same degree, and in the same sense, that other religious systems emphasize other-worldliness.

Jesus has become an idol, if you will, our focus of attention, our focus of worship, and it seems that very few think about God anymore. Seldom do we hear anyone speak of the glory of God, his grandeur and mercy, the holiness of God, and the other many attributes and characteristics of God. There is very little talk about God anymore.

Please understand that I am not trying to lessen the importance of Jesus. What I am trying to do is emphasize that, in all of the teachings of Jesus recorded for us in the gospels, his focus is not upon himself, what he is, what he is doing, or what he is to become. Additionally, Jesus has very little to say about God and, in particular, the worship of God. We do not read in the gospels of Jesus instructing people how they are to worship God, what they are to pray, or to sing, or what they are to do when they come together.

My point is that, in the teachings of Jesus, there is not all that much emphasis upward. When the disciples come to Jesus and ask him to teach them how to pray, Jesus gives them some very specific instructions as to where the focus of those who are part of his movement is to be.

Dr. Brad Young has published an excellent book on this subject, *The Jewish Background to the Lord's Prayer.* In his book, Dr. Young points out that the emphasis in the prayer that Jesus taught his disciples to pray is outward, not just thy kingdom come, but let your kingdom be spread abroad over the whole earth in such a way that God may begin to rule in the lives of more and more people. Let those who are being ruled by God demonstrate his rule in their lives in action.

The action of those who are a part of the kingdom of God, who are being ruled by God, is outward in acts of *tzedakah* toward their fellow man. What is *tzedakah*? We translate it very frequently in the English as righteousness, or as almsgiving, or charity; but, it is a word that really defies translation into English, a word pregnant with meaning.

In *Deuteronomy*, chapter 15, verse 7 ff., we read:

> If there is among you a poor man, one of your kinsmen in any of the towns of your land which the Lord your God gives you, you shall not harden your mind and heart or close your hand to your poor brother, but you shall open your hand wide to him, and shall surely lend him sufficient for his need, which he lacks. Beware lest there be a base thought in your mind and heart and you say, 'the seventh year, or the year of release, is at hand,' and your eye be evil against your poor brother, and you give him nothing, and he cry to the Lord against you, and it be sin in you. You shall give to him freely without begrudging it, because for this the Lord will bless you in all your work and in all you undertake. For the poor will never cease out of the land; therefore, I command you, you shall open wide your hand to your brother, to your needy, and to your poor in your land (*Deuteronomy* 15:7-11 Amplified).

*Torah* insists that the poor and needy be remembered. The biblical text expected the people of God to be aware of the need of the poor and the stranger. In chapter 10 of *Deuteronomy*, verse 19, it gives the reason why. "Therefore, love the stranger and sojourner for you were strangers and sojourners in the land of Egypt." *Tzedakah* is not an option. It is a responsibility, an obligation, but notice, an obligation not without promise. "The Lord will bless you in all your work and in all to which you put your hand."

*Tzedakah* is an attribute of God himself. In *Deuteronomy* 10:17-18 we read, "For the Lord your God is God of gods and Lord of lords, the great, the mighty, the terrible God, who is not partial and takes no bribe. He executes justice for the fatherless and widow and loves the stranger, (or temporary resident), and gives him food and clothing." The woman of valor in *Proverbs* 31:20 was the one who "stretched out her hand to the poor and needy." In *Proverbs* 19:17, charity to the poor is equated to lending to God and the good deed He will repay.

However, there is no one word in the biblical text that expresses this idea of man's responsibility to his fellow man. The rabbis adopted *tzedakah* to describe it. Another closely related and widely used word is *chesed*. *Chesed* is frequently translated as loving-kindness, and it is used widely in the biblical text to refer to physical aid or lending assistance of one kind or another apart from giving money or food to assist the poor and needy.

Unfortunately, we have been guilty of equating righteousness (*tzedakah* and/or *chesed*) with holiness, or spirituality, being in a right relationship with God. We have never quite understood that in order to be in a right relationship with God, one must first be in a right relationship with his fellow man.

It is interesting to note that the rabbis saw *tzedakah* not as a favor they were doing for the poor but as a favor the poor were doing for them because, they said, the poor man does more for the householder in accepting alms than the householder does for the poor man by giving him alms. In accepting the alms, the poor man gives the householder an opportunity to perform a good deed, or a *mitzvah*. Since *tzedakah* is considered a biblical commandment, the rabbis found it necessary, as in the case of every other commandment, to define it in detail.

How does one perform a *mitzvah* of *tzedakah*? Who is obligated to give? Who is eligible to receive? How much should be given? In what manner should it be given? Throughout the *Talmud*, we find these various laws on how to give and how to receive *tzedakah*. Everyone was obligated to give, even the person who himself was dependent upon acts of *tzedakah* was obliged to give to one who was less fortunate than himself.

Acts of *tzedakah* toward a non-Jew were just as obligatory as they were to a Jew. That is, even if one was not a member of the house of God, or the family of Israel, even if one was considered to be a Gentile, a pagan, or an outsider, he was still worthy to receive acts of *tzedakah* in order to preserve good relations.

Another interesting point of law is that women were always to take precedence over men in receiving *tzedakah*. One's poor relations were to come before strangers. The poor of your own community come before the poor of another.

Maimonides took all of these various laws of *Talmud* and the *Mishnah* and codified them. He listed eight ways *tzedakah* was to be performed. They are progressively more virtuous, each one becoming more virtuous than the other. As you read, reflect back on some of the sayings of Jesus relative to the subject and see if it does not ring a bell in your mind.

1. To give, but sadly (Remember, Jesus taught that the Lord loves a cheerful giver.)
2. To give less than is fitting, but in good humor.
3. To give, but only after having been asked to.
4. To give before being asked.
5. To give in such a manner that the donor does not know who the recipient is.
6. To give in such a manner that the recipient does not know who the donor is.
7. To give in such a way that neither the donor nor the recipient knows the identity of the other.
8. To help the poor to rehabilitate themselves by lending them money, taking them into partnership, employing them, or giving them work, for in this way, the end is achieved without any loss of self-respect at all (Maimonides, *Yad Mattenot Aniyyim* 10:7-12).

Maimonides continued that when necessary, accepting charity is perfectly legitimate. Do not be embarrassed. Do not be ashamed, because no shame attaches to the poor who are otherwise unable to support themselves. However, one is advised to do everything within one's power to keep from accepting charity if at all possible, and so the quote from *Jeremiah* 17:7, "Blessed is the man that trusts in the Lord." In other words, even if a person has to endure some kind of physical suffering such as hunger, if he can just go as far as he can without accepting charity, it will be a special blessing for him if he trusts God instead of others. But, if there is no other option available, then there is no shame in accepting charity.

One important principle of charity is that it was to begin at home. The broad family circle was the primary unit for receiving relief, and beyond the family circle was the community to which the individual belonged. There is, however, a higher form of *tzedakah* – *gemilut hasadim*, which means the practice of charity. It comes from the Hebrew word *chesed*. In the *Mishnah, Order Nezikin, Tractate Avot*, Chapter 1, *Mishnah* 2, Simon the Just was one of the last survivors of the Great Assembly (circa 200 BCE). He used to say, "Upon three things is the world based, upon the law, upon divine service, and upon the practice of charity (*gemilut hasadim*)."

*Gemilut hasadim* might be translated as the practice of acts of loving-kindness. It is the most comprehensive and fundamental of all Jewish social virtues. It encompasses the whole range of the duties man has toward his fellow man. In the *Chapters of the Fathers*, or *Pirke Avot*, from which we just quoted, the statement of Simon the Just comes immediately after the opening statement of Chapter 1, *Mishnah* 1. "Moses received the list from Sinai and handed it down to Joshua, and Joshua to the elders, and the elders to the prophets, and the prophets handed it down to the men of the Great Assembly." They said three things. "Be deliberate in judgment, raise up many disciples, and make a fence around the law."

Make a fence around the law means to set boundaries. That is, this is as far as one can go and beyond that, one cannot go. Then, the statement of Simon the Just immediately follows. In *Mishnah* 3, Antigonus of Soco received from Simon the Just. In *Mishnah* 4, Jose ben Joezer and Jose ben Jochanan received from them. In other words, we have a principle being established of the continuation of tradition being passed from one generation to the next that continues uninterrupted from Moses onward.

The principle of *gemilut hasadim* is one of the earliest individual rabbinic statements in *Mishnah* and serves as one of the three pillars of Judaism. *Gemilut hasadim*, however, encompasses a much wider range of human activity and loving-kindness than just simple acts of *tzedakah*. For example, *tzedakah*, or charity, can be given only with one's money; whereas, *gemilut hasadim* can be both the giving of money and/or personal service. Charity can be given only to the poor. *Gemilut hasadim* can be given to anyone.

Charity can be given only to the living. *Gemilut hasadim* can be given to both the living and the dead, e.g., helping a lame man over some kind of an obstacle would be considered an act of *gemilut hasadim* and not merely an act of charity. A gift given to a poor man may be an act of charity but not necessarily an act of *gemilut hasadim*. The same act of giving charity to the poor, but giving it with a smile and/or a word of encouragement or cheer, would raise the act from charity to *gemilut hasadim*. The rabbis continued that the only provable example of genuine altruistic *gemilut hasadim* is paying respect to the dead or assisting in the burial of the dead, because it is obvious there are no ulterior motives on the part of the doer in expecting to receive something back from the recipient.

In *Ecclesiastes Rabbah* 7 and 1, it says, "He who denies the duty of *gemilut hasadim* denies the fundamental tenet of Judaism." Again, we note that the foundation stone of biblical faith is not man's actions upward toward God but, rather, his responsibilities to his fellow man. We will see this idea repeated over and over again in the teachings, or sayings, of the rabbis we are going to be noting as we compare their teachings in *Pirke Avot*, the *Chapters of the Fathers*, with the teachings of Jesus. The similarity in teaching, as well as style, is both dramatic and important. Jesus says almost nothing about how to worship God, about how to pray, about ritual, or religion, form, ceremony, sacrifice, or service upward toward God. When Jesus looks out over the multitude and begins to teach, he sees beyond the multitudes and sees the world. His injunction, his commission, to the multitudes is to "Go and proclaim the good news" or as it is frequently quoted, "Go and preach the gospel."

That is an important statement, but what does it mean? In *Matthew* 3, we read, "In those days came John the Baptist preaching in the wilderness of Judah and saying, 'Repent, for the kingdom of heaven is at hand.'" That was his message. The kingdom of God is at hand. What did he mean? In Chapter 4, verse 23, we read, "Jesus went about all Galilee teaching in their synagogues and preaching the gospel of the kingdom."

Notice the next phrase, "And healing all manner of sickness and all manner of disease among the people."

The gospel of the kingdom is not a message about getting to go to heaven. It is not a message for the hereafter, or the world to come. It is a message for today. It is a message that men and women can come in contact with the power of the living God who breaks through the space time continuum to meet them at the point of their human need. It is a message that men and women can be delivered, healed, made whole, by the power of the living God. That was the "good news." That was the gospel of the kingdom.

God can and will penetrate into this space time continuum in which we live and, in Him, one can live in wholeness, in peace, in happiness, and in joy, now, in this world. That was, and is, the basic difference between western Christianity, as it would later develop, and biblical faith.

Biblical faith is very much a religion of today; whereas, western Christianity developed along the lines of the oriental, mystical religions of that day which were other-worldly. The desire was to escape this physical body that entraps us and to ascend to another-worldly state of nirvana, or paradise – Christianity's "pie-in-the-sky by-and-by." But that is not biblical faith.

That is not the teaching of the rabbis, nor is it the teaching of Jesus. Jesus taught, "Take no thought saying what shall we eat or what shall we drink or with what shall we be clothed... but you seek first the kingdom of God and His righteousness (*tzedakah*), and all these things shall be added unto you. Take therefore no thought for the morrow..." (*Matthew* 6:31-34).

Notice that Simon was called "the Just," Shimon Hatzadik, and he said, "Upon three things does the world stand, the law, divine service, and *gemilut hasadim*." Antigonus of Soco received from Simon the Just, and he used to say, "Be not like servants that minister to the master on the condition of receiving a reward, but be like servants that minister to the master without the condition of receiving a reward and let the fear of heaven be upon you."

Here we see *gemilut hasadim* defined. And where did Antigonus get his teaching, or tradition? From Simon. And from where did Simon get his? From the prophets, and the prophets from the elders, the elders from Joshua, Joshua from Moses, and Moses from God. Here is the point. When we read the teachings of these men, it is like we are hearing God speak. This is not just some extra-biblical commentary by some uninspired Jewish rabbis. Note the similarity between the teaching of the rabbis and the *Chapters of the Fathers* and the teachings of Jesus. They are so strongly similar that we cannot account for it on the grounds of simple coincidence.

It is interesting and fascinating that many times these individuals will be identified with a particular city or location so that we can pinpoint where they came from, where they lived, where they worked. Here is an interesting statement from Jose ben Joezer, "Let your house be a meeting house for the wise and sit amidst the dust of their feet and drink in their words thirstily." (*Avot* 1:4). The passage is difficult to translate into English and, as translated, presents a picture of the rabbi, or the wise man, with his students sitting at his feet.

The *Mishnah* emphasizes that one's house should be a meeting place for the sages and then the Hebrew says, "...and cover yourselves with the dust of their feet and drink in their words thirstily." In biblical times, the picture of the sage, or the teacher, or the rabbi, was one of a peripatetic, charismatic figure who moved from place to place. Following along behind him was his little group of students, or disciples. If one wanted to study with one of these rabbis, or teachers, one had to follow after them.

Remember the call of Jesus to his disciples? "Come. Follow me." In Jesus' day, if you wanted to study with one of these rabbis, or teachers, you had to follow after them – and they did not have paved roads. They only had little paths, and if any of you have been in Israel, you know that in the dry season, from mid-April to mid-November when it never rains, everything is covered with a fine dust. If you follow after somebody, or walk behind them, it is not very long before you are literally eating from the dust of their feet. This gives you a wonderful picture of the peripatetic rabbi or teacher, of which Jesus was one.

Notice the injunction, "...drink in their words thirstily." That is, listen to what they say. Give heed to what they say. In *Matthew* 17:5, when the heavens opened up and God spoke forth out of a cloud, his words were, "This is my beloved son in whom I am well pleased. Hear ye Him." The phrases, "Drink in their words thirstily," and "Hear Him," are synonymous, i.e., listen to what they say. Listen with the idea not just of hearing but of obeying. In other words, do what they say.

We are reminded of the words of another sage who wrote, "Be ye doers of the word and not hearers only, deceiving your own selves, for if any be a hearer of the word and not a doer, he is like unto a man beholding his natural face in a glass for he beholds himself and goes his way and straightway forgets what manner of man he is. But whoso looks into the perfect law of liberty and continues therein, not being a forgetful hearer but a doer of the word, this man shall be blessed in his deed." (*James* 1:22-25).

In summary, there is an underlying, overriding, and yet simple, theme that serves as the foundational theme of biblical faith. That theme is *tzedakah*, frequently translated as righteousness, or purity, but in reality a word that means so much more.

It is difficult for us to understand or to grasp the implication of the word until we listen carefully to the teachings of Jesus and his contemporaries. In order to begin to grasp the full implications, we must first understand that biblical faith is not so much man's actions directed upward toward God but rather his actions directed outward toward his fellow man.

In *Mishnah* 5, Jose ben Jochanan of Jerusalem said, "Let your house be open wide and let the needy be members of your household." Notice again the emphasis being placed upon man's responsibility to his fellow man.

## CHAPTER 2
# TEACHING, TITHING AND SILENCE

There is something to which I would like to call your attention. To me, it is so exciting! Notice as we read through the pages in *Mishnah* that it is specifying the city from which each of the rabbis come, i.e., Antigonus of Socho, or Jose ben Joezer of Zeredah. And in *Mishnah* 6 we read of Nittai the Arbelite.

To me, this is one of the exciting, thrilling things about the *Bible*, about the *Mishnah*, even historical documents such as the writings of Josephus, in that they are talking about places, cities, countries, empires, mountains, rivers, kings, kingdoms, etc., all of which can be verified historically and/or archaeologically to establish the authenticity of the document, the accuracy of the author.

I am sure that I got more excited reading this material because I have been there. I have been to the cities, the countries, the historical and archaeological sites, and as I read, just one word will elicit a mental and emotional image that immediately takes me to that place. Arbela, e.g., is one of the great historical sites on the edge of the Sea of Galilee along the southwestern shore bordering the Arbel Valley which, in turn, borders the Valley of Ginnosar that marks the dividing line between lower Galilee to the south, and upper Galilee to the north.

Just one word can elicit an explosion of mental images. You can see the geographic area, the archaeological site, etc., which, in turn, leads to stories from historical writers such as Josephus, for example, who talks in detail about Arbela during the first revolt and the time of Herod Agrippa.

Nittai, the Arbelite, also said, "Keep thee far from an evil neighbor, and associate not thyself with the godless, and abandon not belief in retribution." Does this call to your mind the words of Paul in *1 Thessalonians* 5:22 when he writes, "Abstain from all appearances of evil."? Do not associate with the godless, and even in the midst of seeming despair, do not abandon the idea of the final judgment and the justice of God. Vengeance belongs to God. One day, there will be a judgment and men will be brought into account for their deeds. Regardless of what it is that is happening to you, do not abandon the idea of the ultimate judgment and justice of God.

In *Mishnah* 11, Chapter 1, Abtalion said, "Ye Sages, be cautious of your words lest ye incur the penalty of exile and be banished to a place of evil waters whereof the disciples that come after you drink and die and the heavenly name be profaned." This is an interesting *Mishnah* that, if you know nothing of Jewish history, it will make little sense and will remain a mystery to you. Abtalion enjoins the Sages, the religious leaders, to be cautious in their teachings. Teaching should be so precise that it leaves no room for misinterpretation, or misunderstanding, or could possibly lead from misunderstanding into heresy.

Incurring the penalty of exile and being banished to the place of evil waters is a specific reference to the city of Alexandria in Egypt. During the time of Jeremiah the prophet, and before the destruction of the Temple by Nebuchadnezzer of Babylon in 586 BCE, many of the Jews fled from Israel to Egypt. Some even fled as far down the Nile as Aswan, and to the little island in the middle of the Nile known as Elephantine, or Yeb.

At Elephantine, there was a large Jewish community which had constructed a temple oriented toward the Temple in Jerusalem. In the archaeological excavations at Elephantine, many letters were found written on papyrus that were letters of correspondence between the Jews at Elephantine and the Jews back in Jerusalem.

Some of the individuals mentioned in the books of Ezra and Nehemiah are mentioned in the Elephantine papyri. Many of the Jews that were not taken into captivity fled before the destruction to Alexandria. During the time of Alexander the Great, the Greek or Hellenistic period, the Hellenistic culture influenced these Jews to the degree that by the $3^{rd}$ century BCE, they no longer understood Hebrew.

Thus, there was the necessity for the translation of the Hebrew Scriptures into Greek. That translation was probably finished during the reign of Ptolemy Lagos about 285 BCE and is known today as the *Septuagint*, sometimes abbreviated as LXX, or the 70. Tradition has it that it was translated by 70 learned Jews. Alexandria is mentioned as a place of exile because it was there, according to the Jews back in the land of Israel, that Hellenistic Jewry corrupted Jewish orthodoxy and promoted heresy.

To illustrate this point, commentators frequently refer to *Mishnah* 3 of this chapter and state that the teaching of Antigonus of Socho was misrepresented by two of his disciples, Zadok and Boethus, who taught that there is no immortality of the soul and no reward in the world to come.

This heresy led to the establishment of the sects of the Sadducees and the Boethusians. We now learn how the sect of the Sadducees originated. The admonition of Abtalion should be heeded by every teacher today. Be careful what you say. Be careful what you teach. We need to be very careful to make sure that what we say is said in such a way as to be so explicit that it cannot be misunderstood. That is not always easy. There are times when one's audience might not have a sufficient background to understand what is being said. We need to be aware of our audience and sure of our words.

In *Mishnah* 12, we are told that Hillel and Shammai received their tradition from the foregoing Sages. Hillel and Shammai are the last and most renowned of the *zugot*, or pairs. Notice once again how each receives from his predecessor so that all goes back not just to Moses but all the way back to God.

Hillel and Shammai were both contemporary with Jesus and considered two of the greatest Sages of their day, representing two different schools of Jewish thought. Hillel, in most instances, might be considered more liberal. The school of Shammai, on the other hand, might appear more conservative.

I personally believe we could identify a third school of thought as the school of Jesus – all three contemporary with one another in the 1st century. I believe that can be established from some of the teachings of Jesus when He runs headlong into a controversy between the two different schools, the school of Hillel and the school of Shammai.

To illustrate that point, we can note Jesus' teaching about divorce in *Matthew* 5:31 when He says, "Whoever shall put away his wife let him give her a bill of divorcement." Jesus is quoting from *Deuteronomy* 24:1. He said, "You have heard that it has been said, 'You shall not commit adultery.'" He goes on to say, "But I say unto you that whosoever puts away his wife save for the cause of fornication causes her to commit adultery, and whosoever shall marry her that is divorced shall commit adultery."

I believe there has been more guilt and condemnation brought upon the people of God from misunderstanding and mistranslation of this passage of scripture than perhaps any other saying or teaching of Jesus. I have actually seen congregations split apart over the subject of divorce. Murder, theft, whatever, God can forgive it all; but in some peculiar way, divorce becomes the unpardonable sin.

What is Jesus really saying? In order to understand what is happening, we have to see Jesus coming into conflict with the school of Hillel and the school of Shammai over the subject of divorce and remarriage.

In *Everyman's Talmud* by A. Cohen, 166, we read that in the 1st century of the present era, the schools of Shammai and Hillel took opposite views of the biblical text in *Deuteronomy* 24:1 which allows a man to send his wife away if she find no favor in his eyes because he has found some "unseeming thing" in her. The phrase "unseeming thing" is literally the nakedness of a thing which the school of Shammai explained to mean that a man may not divorce his wife unless he discovered her to be unfaithful to him.

Hillel, on the other hand, declared he may divorce her even if she spoiled his cooking. From the words, "...if she find no favor in his eyes," Rabbi Akiva argued that he may divorce her even if he found another woman more beautiful than she (*Order Nashim, Tractate Gittin* 9:10).

The more lenient opinion of Hillel was adopted as law so that in Jesus' day a man could put away his wife even if he did not like her looks. Here we have an example of something Jesus taught when he talked about the scribes and the Pharisees teaching for commandment the traditions of men. This was not a commandment. In Jesus' day, Jewish law was very specific. There were reasons whereby a man could put away his wife and a wife could put away a husband. It was specific in law. Everybody knew it.

While the details are beyond the scope of this study, what is important to understand is that in Jesus' day there was a certain body of law that specified why a man or a woman would be justified in going to a rabbinic court and being granted a bill of divorcement. Bet-Shammai (the school of Shammai) said he could do so only for adultery, and Hillel said he could put away his wife for any reason. In the midst of this controversy, Jesus taught that a man is not to put away his wife for any reason except for the cause of fornication.

What does he mean? Fornication is illicit sexual relations by unmarrieds. In biblical times, virginity was held in high regard, and the marriage was arranged by the bridegroom and the father of the bride, and the contract, called a *ketubah*, was written and signed. In the contract, it specified, as many as four times, that the bridegroom was paying such-and-such a price for the virgin daughter of so-and-so in lieu of her virginity. The price was agreed upon. The amount was paid.

When the ceremony took place, the bride and groom retired to a special place to consummate their marriage. The marriage would be consummated on a special sheet. The next morning, that sheet would be displayed publicly with blood on it to serve as a testimony to all the guests at the wedding feast that the woman had, indeed, been a virgin. That special sheet was known, from *Deuteronomy*, Chapter 22, as "the tokens of her virginity." It would be kept with her for the rest of her life and, according to Jewish law, if at any time the husband accused his wife of not being a virgin when they married, all she had to do was bring out the "tokens of her virginity" and show it to a rabbi (or his equivalent), and her husband could never divorce her for any reason because he had falsely accused her.

Jesus enters into the midst of this argument and He says that the only reason whereby a man who is in a proper relationship with both God and his wife should ever put away his wife is if the marriage contract was falsified which would, in turn, render the union null and void, and that is all He has to say about it. He does not go into all of the exceptions because He does not have to. They are already specified by law. He is simply engaging in the controversy between the school of Hillel and the school of Shammai, and He enters into the controversy by setting things into His own unique perspective.

What does it mean when Jesus says that if a man puts away his wife and somebody marries her that he causes her to commit adultery? Because, if she had been put away for no legal reason, she would still be considered to be married. The onus, again, is on the husband who unjustly puts his wife away.

Frankly, this passage has no practical application insofar as our society and our culture is concerned today. To take this controversy out of context and to impose spiritual bondage on individuals in the congregation of God is to render them a grave disservice.

What is exciting to me is that, when you know these things, when you have studied it from its historical and cultural perspective, it is liberating. However, here one must again be careful. Many times when someone starts talking about liberty and freedom, people automatically take that to be license to do whatever they want whenever they want. Liberty is not the right to do what you want; it is the right to do what you ought.

Hillel and Shammai said, "Be thou disciples of Aaron, loving peace and pursuing peace, loving your fellow creatures and drawing them nigh to the law." If you look very carefully at this statement, you can see that it is very similar to the statements Jesus makes in the Sermon on the Mount. Love peace...Run after the holiness...and the completeness that only God can give. Love your fellow creatures, those that God has created...and you shall love your neighbor as yourself.

Do you remember when they came to Jesus and asked him which was the greatest commandment of all and He responds, "Love the Lord your God with all your heart, with all your mind, and all your soul, and the second is like unto it; you shall love your neighbor as yourself."? If you love them as yourself, you are going to attempt to bring them into an intimate relationship with God and let Him become a reality in their lives.

One of the most famous of the sayings of Hillel is quoted in *Mishnah* 14, "If I am not for myself, who will be for me, and if I am for mine ownself, what am I? And if not now, when?" Hillel indicates that one can attain true virtue only through his own strivings. No one else can be righteous for you. If one is selfish and disregards others, what kind of man is he? The moral duties and responsibilities that man has to his fellow man must be carried out immediately as the condition or situation arises and not be postponed lest the opportunity to serve others is lost. Selfishness, disregard for others, are not traits of the one who is the child of God and is practicing *tzedakah* or *gemilut hasadim*.

In *Mishnah* 15, Shammai said, "Make the study of the law a fixed duty. Say little and do much and regard every man with cheerful countenance." Notice that the emphasis here is (1) on study; and (2) on actions directed outward toward one's fellow man.

Professor David Flusser of Hebrew University in Jerusalem said in his book, *Jewish Sources in Early Christianity*, 33-34:

> The Pious, to whom Jesus belonged, were not scrupulous in matters of purification. In general, they were opposed to the emphasis put on the study of Torah as a supreme value and, instead, emphasized the importance of good deeds...These Pious opposed the growing tendency toward intellectualism. Indeed, most of the Sages accepted the view of the Pious 'not learning but doing is the chief thing' as stated by Rabbi Shimon ben Gamliel (*Avot* 1:17).

> The tension between good deeds and intellectualism continued until 120 CE when the Sages concluded after long debate between themselves that the study of Torah takes precedence since it leads one to action.

> Jesus always emphasized the importance of action. He commanded his disciples to act according to the ruling of the Pharisees and frequently spoke of doing the will of His father in Heaven. Study always took second place with Jesus although He was far more learned than most people of his social position and, certainly, more learned than Paul, although Paul studied in Jerusalem.

Jesus had a deep and thorough Jewish education and was probably much more knowledgeable in these matters than Paul. It is interesting to see the seeming conflict between the importance of study and the importance of doing developing. Ultimately, as Professor Flusser has pointed out, study is given primary importance because, without knowledge, one does not know what they are supposed to do. So, Shammai says, "Make a study of the law a fixed duty. Say little but do much." Once again, we want to notice the importance that is placed upon action.

Rabban Gamliel said in *Mishnah* 16, "Provide thyself a teacher and relieve thyself of doubt, and accustom not thyself to tithe by conjecture." In this interesting *Mishnah*, Rabban Gamliel mentions the matter of tithing. He implies there must be no guesswork in the offering of the first fruits offering, (*terumah*), and the tithes.

Perhaps we would all do well to heed Gamliel's injunction to provide ourselves with a teacher in the matter of tithing to relieve ourselves not just of doubt but of the erroneous teaching that has been prevalent in the Church for over a thousand years. It is another one of those subjects that has brought a great deal of bondage on the people of God because it has been misinterpreted, taken out of context, and elevated to the stature of an ordinance such as Baptism and the Lord's Supper.

It is important to note that there are actually four different tithes in Judaism, not just one. The first is the *terumah*, or the first fruits offering. The second was the *ma'aser rishon*, or first tithe. The third was the *ma'aser min hama'aser*, the tithe of the tithe, or the tithe from the tithe. Finally, there was the *ma'aser sheni*, or the second tithe.

The tithes were offered during the course of a seven year period, the seventh year known as the Sabbath Year. The tithe was offered only six years out of the seven. The first, second, fourth, and fifth years, the second tithe was taken up to Jerusalem and offered up unto the Lord and then consumed by the people that offered it. After it had been offered to God, they had a big party and enjoyed the offering that obviously God could not eat. On the third and sixth years, the second tithe stayed at home within the walls of the city and was used to take care of the poor, the widows, orphans, and all that were in need.

No one who lived outside of the boundary of Israel was allowed to tithe. It was strictly for the Jew. The interesting question, however, was what was the purpose of the tithe? If we study the subject carefully, we will see this idea of *tzedakah* at the heart and the center of the tithe. Remember, the *terumah*, the first fruits offering, once offered up went to the priests. The first tithe went to the Levites. The Levites offered the tithe from the tithe to the priests, and the second tithe was for the people.

Because the priests and Levites had no inheritance in the land, they were considered to be on a par with the poor and entitled to the support of the community.

The purpose of the tithe was not to support some kind of ecclesiastical establishment but, rather, for the support of the congregation of God.

Tithing, as a matter of law, was first imposed on the Church in the 8th century by Charlemagne, king of the Francs, in one of his Capitularies. From that time until now, we have been taught by religious leaders that the child of God was responsible to give 10% for the support of the religious institution. Notice, however, that in Judaism, the Jew was responsible for approximately 21.7%.

Something must be said at this point about attitude. The real child of God is not responsible for 10%. He was and is responsible for 100%, and he must do and give as God directs in order that the body might be whole.

Rabban Gamliel, in this *Mishnah*, is dealing specifically with the matter of giving, and he says, "If any of you have any questions about how much to give and to whom to give, get yourself a teacher. Call for someone who can give you proper instruction and relieve any doubt as to what your responsibilities are in this matter."

That admonition might have some practical applications for us today. But again, I want you to notice that underlying it all is the idea of reaching outward to meet the needs of people as opposed to reaching upward in worship of God.

Simon, the son of Gamliel, said, "I was brought up all my life among the Sages, and I have found nothing so essentially good as silence, and not the study of the law is of fundamental import but the practice thereof, and whosoever is profuse of words brings sin." In *Proverbs* 17:28, it says, "Even a fool when he holds his peace is considered wise." In other words, when he closes his lips he is esteemed to be a man of understanding.

Jewish literature has a lot to say about knowing when to keep quiet. Even in the matter of prayer, Judaism declares that most people spend too much time praying because most of their prayers are nothing more than whining and begging God for something, or they are vain prayers, or unrighteous prayers, and that, ultimately, the only type of prayer that is effective or enduring is the prayer of thanksgiving.

It is concluded that the highest form of prayer is simply silence for the simple reason that God has a difficult time speaking to you when your mouth is moving. The admonition, therefore, is to sit down, be quiet, and open yourself to hear God speak. Shimon is saying that nothing is so essentially good as silence, and not the study of the law is of fundamental importance, but the practicing of it.

Notice how the Sages are echoing one another and how it all harmonizes completely with the words of Jesus. Would that somehow the people of God could gain understanding of the teachings of Jesus and his contemporaries!

A more detailed study of tithing can be found in my book, *Tithing Giving and Prosperity.*

# CHAPTER 3

# A GOOD EYE

Probably anyone who has ever focused on the teachings of Jesus in any depth is aware that he was a product of the religious milieu that emerged in the 1$^{st}$ century of this present era. The four gospels preserve for us the largest and the best corpus of material relating to the ideas and methods of teaching of the rabbis of that period. As we compare the words of Jesus with the other rabbis of his day, we can begin to understand where some of the ideas originated, the way they were thinking, the themes upon which they were teaching.

*Mishnah* 8 of Chapter 2 mentions Rabbi ben Zakki, who was a very interesting figure in history just prior to the destruction of the Temple. Rabbi ben Zakki realized that the end for the city of Jerusalem and for the Jewish cause was near. He contrived a plan and was carried out of the city of Jerusalem in a coffin as dead. He was carried by the disciples and into the camp of Vespasian, the Roman emperor, and proceeded to prophesy Vespasian's victory. He requested from Vespasian that he be allowed to leave the city of Jerusalem prior to its destruction with his disciples. Vespasian granted him special privileges, and he was allowed to go to Yavne and start an academy.

After the destruction of the Temple in 70 CE, the Sanhedrin was transferred from Jerusalem to Yavne and remained there until it was transferred to the north into Galilee.

Rabbi ben Zakki was the one who, after the destruction of the Temple, formulated the direction that Judaism would take in the future by concluding that the study of Torah, the offering of prayers, and the doing of acts of *tzedakah* took the place of, and even superseded, the sacrifices in the Temple.

In *Mishnah* 8, Rabbi ben Zakki talked about five of his disciples, Eliezer ben Hyrcanus, Rabbi Joshua ben Chananiah, Rabbi Jose the Priest, Rabbi Shimon ben Nathaniel, and Rabbi Elazar ben Arach. He said something about each of them. Hyrcanus was a cemented cistern that does not lose a drop. Happy is the woman that bore Joshua ben Chananiah. Rabbi Jose is a pious man. Nathaniel is the fearer of sin, and Rabbi Elazar ben Arach is a spring flowing with ever sustained strength.

He went on to say that if all these sages were in one scale of a balance and Eliezer Hyrcanus was in the other scale, he would outweigh them all. Why did he say that? What were they talking about? Their spiritual might, wisdom, the depth of their understanding of God and the things of God.

Again he went on to say that, if all the sages of Israel were in one scale of a balance and Hyrcanus was with them, and Elazar Arach was in the other scale, he would outweigh them all. What was it about Arach that made him so unique? Perhaps *Mishnah* 9 will give us the answer. Rabbi Zakki said, "Go forth and see which is the right way whereunto a man should cleave." Rabbi Eliezer said, "A good eye." Do you remember the "good eye"? It means *tzedakah*. It means to be generous.

Without a doubt, the response of the rabbis reflects something of the manner of their way of life, the way they lived for life. Rabbi Joshua said, "A good friend." Rabbi Jose said, "A good neighbor." Rabbi Shimon said, "One who foresees the ultimate consequences of an action."

Rabbi Elazar ben Arach said, "A good heart." Rabbi ben Zakki commended the words of Arach above all of the others for he stated that, "In his words were all of the others included."

If a person has a good heart, all of the other things are going to be included. This theme of the good heart is a recurring theme, both in the Psalms and in the words of Jesus.

Rabbi ben Zakki said to his disciples, "Go forth and see which is the evil road that a man should shun." Eliezer said, "An evil eye." Rabbi Jose said, "An evil neighbor." Rabbi Shimon said, "One that borrows and does not repay, for he who borrows from man is as one who borrows from the Omnipresent, blessed be He." As it is said, "The wicked borroweth and payeth not again, but the righteous dealeth and giveth (*Psalm 37*)." Who are the righteous of *Psalm 37*?

In the Sermon on the Mount, recorded in *Matthew* 5 and following, Jesus said, "Blessed are the meek for they shall inherit the earth." Where did Jesus get that idea? Who are the meek? What does it mean to be meek? If we did not know that Jesus was a rabbi, speaking Hebrew, using rabbinic methods in his teaching, hinting back at something that has already been said or written, and that his listeners basically have all of this material memorized, we would not understand.

Meek, to us, basically means some kind of a "Casper Milquetoast" sort of character. Or, it could mean humble, or weak. Jesus is quoting from *Psalm 37:11*. The meek shall inherit the earth. Notice in *Psalm 37*, "The arms of the wicked shall be broken, but the Lord upholds the consistently righteous." The wicked borrows and pays not again, but the uncompromisingly righteous deals kindly and gives. Again, we see this idea of *tzedakah*, of generosity rising to the fore.

Who will inherit the earth? The uncompromisingly righteous. Who deals kindly and gives? The uncompromisingly righteous. Who shall inherit the land and dwell upon it forever? The uncompromisingly righteous. Who are the meek? The uncompromisingly righteous. It has nothing to do with weakness or even humility.

Rabbi Elazar said, "A wicked heart," and again was commended above the others, for in his words were included the others. Once again, we are reminded of the words of Jesus in *Matthew* 5:8, "Blessed are the pure in heart for they shall see God." In *Matthew* 15:18, "...those things which proceed out of the mouth come forth from the heart and they defile the man, for out of the heart proceed evil thoughts, murders, adulteries, fornication, etc. These are the things that defile the man."

Notice the vast scope of theology involved in the theme, a good heart and an evil heart. As we look at some of the statements of Jesus and other of the rabbis of his day, we see how this thought is echoed over and over again. In *Mishnah* 10, notice how statements are appearing in triplets. Each said three things. "Let the honor of your fellowman be as precious to you as your own." "Be not easily moved to wrath," and "repent one day before your death." This is Rabbi Eliezer, and the statement, "Repent one day before your death," was one of his principal themes. His students would ask, "But, Rabbi, how can we do that? One does not know when they are going to die." Rabbi Eliezer said, "That is the point. You do not know when you are going to die; therefore, one needs to be in a continual state of repentance."

I want to say something here that I believe to be of the utmost significance to us all. Not long ago, I had a young man come up to me and ask a question relative to *Bible* prophecy and end-time events. He wanted to know what the Jews would have to say on this particular subject. I asked him, "Are you sure you really want to know?" He looked puzzled, and I explained.

There is an interesting passage in the *Mishnah* in *Order Moed* and in *Tractate Chagigah*, Chapter 2, *Mishnah* 1. It reads, "Whoever puts his mind to these four matters, it would be better for him if he had not come into this world – what is up above, what is down below, what is out in the future, and what is in the past."

The commentary in Blackman's *Mishnah* continues that, "Any discussion on these four subjects is nothing more than useless speculation and idle prognostication that serve no useful academic purpose but only causes a falling away from true biblical faith."

We hear so much in Christianity today about *Bible* prophecy, the Ark of the Covenant, the ashes of the red heifer, end-time events, that the Lord is coming soon. Let me shock you with a statement. If you believe that the Lord is coming soon, your theology is out of kilter. Not only that, but it is a dangerous theology. Here is why. If you believe that the Lord is coming soon, i.e., sometime out in the very near future, as in that He is going to come during the Feast of Trumpets in September of 2013. He was, as some of you may recall, supposed to do that in 1988. Maybe our calculation was off a little, and He is going to do it in 2013, so I have from now until September of 2013 to live the "good life." I will go out and get a new Cadillac and will not have to make the first payment for 90 days. I can do whatever I want to do because I know it is going to be during the Feast of Trumpets in 2013; so, I have plenty of time to do what I want and repent just before He comes.

Do you want to know something? People were doing just that all over the country after the appearance of the book, *88 Reasons Why The Rapture Will Be in 1988*. People were so convinced that it was true that they actually had their animals put to sleep because they did not want them left behind – all kinds of crazy things. You see, if your theology is that the Lord is coming soon, how out of kilter one can get.

Nowhere in the entire *Bible* does it talk about the Lord coming "soon." It does say that the coming of the Son of Man in His glory is going to be as a thief in the night at a time when you think not. His coming is going to be sudden, not soon, and the injunction is, "Therefore, be ready because at a time when you think not, the Son of Man cometh."

This was also the injunction of Rabbi Eliezer. "Repent one day before you die." Since you do not know when you are going to die, you need to be in a constant state of repentance as no man knows the day or the hour, and we might add, nor the year of the Lord's coming. One needs continually to be ready.

*Mishnah* 11 is very short. Rabbi Joshua said, "The evil eye," the evil inclination, and the hatred of one's fellow creatures puts a man out of the world. The 'evil eye' we know is an idiom for miserliness, or stinginess. But what about the evil inclination? Judaism has a lot to say about the evil inclination, or the *yetzer hara*.

In Judaism, as opposed to many Christian denominations, man is born basically good and created in the image of God. Because man was created in the image of God, he was created with free will, with the ability to choose. Man was something more than an automaton because, in order to be created in the image and likeness of God, he had to be created with the ability to choose either good or evil.

Judaism teaches that man was created with both the *yetzer hatov*, the good inclination, and the *yetzer hara*, the evil inclination. The evil inclination is that part of man that leads him to do all kinds of things that we would say were transgressions of the will of God. The good impulse controls the righteous; the evil impulse controls the wicked. Man, created in the image and likeness of God, is born with both.

The common opinion was that the evil impulse is the disposition of the human being which results from natural instincts, one of them being sexual desire. Sexual sins were declared to be governed by the evil impulse. However, since it was God who created man as he did and commanded him to "be fruitful and to multiply," the evil impulse is not essentially bad as God creates only what is good. It is evil only insofar as it is misused. As it was explained, "Is not the evil very good?" The answer is given, "Were it not for that impulse, man would not build a house, marry a wife, beget children, or conduct business affairs." So, the evil impulse, if properly controlled and channeled, is considered to be good.

We see something of this idea of the evil impulse with Paul in one of his statements when he says, "The good that I would I do not do, and the bad things I do not want to do, I find myself doing." Here is an interesting question. Upon whom would he put the blame for those bad things that he did? The devil? Did the devil make him do the bad things? Was his 'thorn in the flesh' a demon from which he needed deliverance?

Although I do not intend to delve deeply into the subject, I think it is fitting that I at least call to your mind some of the misunderstandings and abuses that are current in some Christian circles today. It is popular and quite easy for us to blame our misdeeds on the devil. "The devil made me do it!" You may be surprised to learn that in Judaism, there is no concept of a devil as being a separate entity co-equal with God and warring against God. That particular theological concept is known as Dualism, and it basically creeps into both Judaism, and later into Christianity, through the Zoroastrianism of Persia from the 4th century BCE and following.

In the *Bible*, the devil, or *hasatan*, the accuser, was a created being, created by God and subject to do his will. Throughout the course of biblical history until the 4th and the 5th century BCE, you read nothing about demons, devils, demonology. It is not until much later that these ideas and concepts began to creep into Judaism, to a degree, and to a much larger degree into Christianity. Much of what we attribute to demons is simply the *yetzer hara* and, if we want victory over it, we are not going to get it by going through deliverance 49 times.

The way to get victory over those things that afflict and hinder is by taking control and bringing it into subjection to the *yetzer hatov*. It necessitates repenting and turning from it. It is an action that comes from within us. Unfortunately, most people want the easy way out.

Someone can pray for you until you fall over in a dead faint, but nothing is going to happen until you want it to happen, until you take control. I really despair as I go around the country and see the immaturity of many of God's people. They are focusing all of their attention on the devil and deliverance, deliverance services, casting out devils.

There is something I have noticed. Wherever you see people focusing all their time and attention on the devil and on deliverance, you are going to see people who are immature in almost every other way as well. The more knowledgeable, the more mature an individual is, the more in control they are of their own lives and their own impulses. Many times, we want to attribute to a devil or to a demon something from without that is nothing more than a part of our own nature, something that is within. If we want to get the victory over it, we are going to have to take control over it. There may be instances when we need outside help, but it will be more of a professional type rather than going through some process of deliverance to be released from some demon over and over again.

Here we see an indication in the saying of Rabbi Joshua, "The evil eye," stinginess, miserliness, the evil inclination – they go together hand-in-hand with the hatred of one's fellow man and put a man out of the world – out of this world and the world to come. When we look at the nature of man, we have to look inside ourselves, at our moral fiber. We all have an inclination to do good and an inclination to do evil. A lack of moral fiber would be yielding to the evil inclination.

Rabbi Jose sums it up in *Mishnah* 12 when he says, "Let the property of thy fellow man be as dear to thee as thy own, and qualify thyself for the study of the law for the knowledge of it is an heritage of thine, and let all your deeds be done for the sake of heaven," in other words, selflessly and without ulterior, selfish motives.

## CHAPTER 4

# THE WILL OF THE FATHER

In Chapter 3, *Mishnah* 3, Rabbi Simon said, "If three have eaten at one table and have not spoken there words of the law, it is as if they have eaten of sacrifices of the dead, as it is said, 'For all their tables are full of vomit and filthiness; the Omnipresent is not in their thoughts.'" (*Isaiah* 28:8). "But if three have eaten at one table and have spoken over it matters concerning the law, it is as though they had eaten from the table of the Omnipresent, blessed be He, as it is said, and he says unto me, 'This is the table that is before the eternal.'" (*Ezekiel* 41:22).

The table in this *Mishnah* refers to the altar of God in the Holy of Holies. Once we take a step back and look very carefully at this *Mishnah* we can see the importance that is placed upon study and learning, rather than upon jesting, or even good manners, when one comes around the table to receive from God's abundance. I remember what I used to do and how I used to be, so it is easy for me to overlook immaturity. Frankly, however, I find it rather humorous when Christians come around the table and feel they just cannot eat until they pray and bless the food. In Judaism, you do not bless the food, you bless God. God is the one who has provided the sustenance, and so it is God that we are to bless for his provision. Actually, I have seen some food that I thought needed to be blessed!

However, God is the one who has provided, so, when his people come around the table, prayer and seriousness sanctify the dining table as though it were the altar of God. It is the appropriate time and the appropriate place to be discussing the things of God – and the appropriate time and appropriate place to bless Him and to thank Him for his provision.

In *Mishnah* 5, Chapter 3, Rabbi Nechunia ben Hakanah said, "Whosoever accepts the yoke of the law, from him shall be removed the yoke of the kingdom and the yoke of mundane care. But he that casts off from him the yoke of the law, upon him shall be laid the yoke of the kingdom and the yoke of worldly care." Unfortunately, most Christians have in their minds the mistaken idea that the law is a burden, or the keeping of the law is some kind of a yoke, a burden to be borne.

It is obvious from what we know of rabbinic literature that there were certain of the Pharisees who did believe that the weight of the law was like a yoke. They went around bowed over as though they were carrying a heavy burden. It seems apparent that it is to these individuals Jesus is referring when he says, "Come unto me all ye that labor and are heavy laden, and I will give you rest."

However, the greater number of the Jews did not see the law as a burden at all, but something to be borne proudly and joyfully – with happiness. The keeping of the law was an occasion for joy and festivity. I believe Jesus was alluding to that in *Matthew* 11:28-31 when he says "Come unto me all ye that labor and are heavy laden, and I will give you rest. Take my yoke upon you and learn of me for I am meek and lowly at heart."

Here we have again the word meek, and lowly, or humble. Remember from *Psalm 37* that meek means uncompromisingly righteous. How were the uncompromisingly righteous characterized in *Psalm 37*? They were those that dealt kindly and gave. Here, again, we see this recurring theme of *tzedakah*, the central theme of Jesus' teaching. His burden, yoke, is easy. His burden light because it is the burden of a good heart, of *tzedakah* – the burden of generosity. The burden of being consistently and uncompromisingly righteous is easy. The burden of stinginess, of miserliness, of the evil eye – that is a heavy burden.

Do you know something interesting? It is harder to be bad than it is to be good. It even has more of a physiological effect. Whereas, if you are basically a good person, generous, loving, one who loves God and his fellow man, there is no strife, or anger, or frustration, none of the characteristics or qualities that engender within the individual a physiological response that is a detriment to the physical body.

There is a real lesson here, both in this *Mishnah* and in the words of Jesus. The yoke of a good eye and a good heart, the yoke of righteousness, leads to rest for the soul.

In *Mishnah* 15, Chapter 3, it says, "All is foreseen by God, yet freedom of choice is granted; and by grace is the universe changed, yet all is according to the amount of the work." This statement is attributed to Rabbi Akiva. Although it is a very short *Mishnah*, it is pregnant with meaning.

Much has been said in Christian circles about predestination. Whole denominations have been established on the theological foundation of predestination – God has predestined certain individuals for salvation and others to be lost. Although this *Mishnah* is succinct, it nonetheless, in one brief sentence, serves to clarify this point and reflect something to us concerning the nature of God.

Omniscience is foreknowledge, foreknowing. In spite of the fact that God knows all, he has given freedom of choice to man. Man has the capacity to do good or to do evil. In Judaism, it is known as the *yetzer hatov* and the *yetzer hara*, and without the ability to choose, freedom of choice, man would be nothing more than a mere automaton.

By grace, and grace alone, is the universe changed. There is nothing that man could do, nothing that man could ever say, no price that man could ever pay that would be sufficient to repay God for redemption. That was done by grace: God's unmerited favor, in which he did something for us that we could not do for ourselves. He did it because he loved us, and he did it for all mankind.

However, because man has freedom of choice, and because some men choose the right and some choose the wrong, there is one day going to come a time of judgment. In Judaism, there is the concept of varying degrees of rewards. A man is going to be repaid according to the works that are done in the flesh. Rabbi Akiva's statement echoes the words of Paul in *1 Corinthians* 3:11-15, "For other foundation can no man lay than that is laid which is Jesus Christ. Now if any man build upon this foundation, gold, silver, precious stones, wood, hay, stubble, every man's work shall be made manifest: for the day shall declare it, because it shall be revealed by fire, and the fire shall try every man's work of what sort it is. If any man's work abide which he has built thereupon, he shall receive a reward. If any man's work shall be burned, he shall suffer loss, but he himself shall be saved, yet so as by fire."

Notice how fire is used figuratively for judgment, "... fire shall try every man's work..." Paul's statement refers to the righteous only. The righteous do not come under condemnation, but there will be that time when their works will be tried by fire and rewards will be disbursed based upon the works that remain.

Where did this whole idea of predestination arise? In *Romans* 8:29-30, Paul states. "For whom he did foreknow, he also did predestinate to be conformed to the image of his son that he might be the firstborn among many brethren. Moreover, whom he did predestinate, them he also called, and whom he called, them he also justified: and whom he justified, them he also glorified."

What did God predestinate? Simply that those who, according to their free will, chose Him...those he predestined to be conformed to the image of his Son. "He that has seen me has seen the Father." There is nothing in either the *Old Testament* or the *New Testament* that supports the theology of election, that God elected certain people to be saved and elected certain people to be lost and that there is nothing one can do about it, that it all hinges on the caprice of God. That is fatalism. Although fatalism is a fundamental principle of Islam, it has absolutely no foundation in biblical fact.

In *Mishnah* 4, Chapter 4, Rabbi Levitas of Yavne said, "Be exceedingly humble of spirit since the hope of man is but the worm." Rabbi Yochanan ben Baroka said, "Whoever profanes the name of heaven in secret will suffer the penalty therefor in public, and it is all one whether the profanation of the name is committed unwittingly or in willfulness."

Recall from our previous studies that Yavne was the city where Rabbi Yochanan ben Zakki started his academy before the destruction of the Temple and where the Sanhedrin was moved after the destruction of the Temple. Rabbi Levitas said. "Be exceedingly humble in spirit." And do you remember the words of Jesus in *Matthew* 5, in the Sermon on the Mount, and how he begins? "Blessed are the poor in spirit..." These statements are exact parallels. But what is more important is how they reflect the thinking of the rabbis from generation to generation.

How important it is that we study rabbinical literature, the sayings of the rabbis. The way in which they teach, the word pictures they paint, the images upon which they draw, because it gives us an understanding of the words of Jesus, the ideas, the concepts upon which he is drawing. In many instances, without a knowledge of this background, because of the images, the idioms, the metaphors, etc., so widely used by the sages and rabbis, we are unable to understand the depth, the meaning, of the words of Jesus.

"...Poor in spirit..." is parallel to humble in spirit, broken in spirit, which means one who is sorrowful for his sins, who has repented of his sins, who has turned to God, who loves His word and who keeps His commandments. That is what it means to be poor in spirit, or humble in spirit. Rabbi Levitas said, "Be exceedingly humble in spirit since the hope of man is but the worm." That is, that the final end of this world is going to be death. Therefore, one needs to make preparation in this world for the world to come. Rabbi ben Baroka emphasizes the fact that one day all will be brought forth and exposed, whether for the good or for the bad.

In *Matthew* 1:16,17,18, Jesus makes the statement that is echoed in the words of ben Baroka, "Moreover, when you fast be not as the hypocrites of a sad countenance, for they disfigure their faces that they may appear unto men that they fast. Verily, I say unto you that they have their reward but you, when you fast, anoint your head and wash your face that you appear not unto men to fast but unto your Father which is in secret, and your Father which sees in secret shall reward you openly."

In *Mishnah* 5 of Chapter 4, Rabbi Ishmael, the son of Rabbi Baroka, said, "He who learns in order to teach will be granted by heaven the means both to learn and to teach; but he that learns in order to practice, heaven will grant him the opportunity to learn and to teach, to observe and to perform." Study was not just to be studying for the sake of accumulating knowledge, that is, knowledge for knowledge's sake, but that the knowledge one acquires might lead to proper action.

Notice again the emphasis that is placed by the rabbis upon doing. Jesus said, "Not everyone that says unto me 'Lord, Lord,' will enter into the kingdom, but he that does the will of my father which is in heaven." In Jesus' day there was somewhat of a conflict between the sages as to which was the most important, study or doing. Frankly, Jesus never made all that much of a to-do over study. His emphasis was upon doing. It was not until 121 CE that the sages finally concluded that study was more important because it was only through study that one could learn what to do. That is, study led to doing.

This whole idea again is echoed in the words of James in his epistle, Chapter 1:22-24, "But be ye doers of the word and not hearers only, deceiving your own selves. For if any be a hearer of the word and not a doer, he is like unto a man beholding his natural face in a glass. For he beholds himself and goes his way and straightway forgets what manner of man he was."

In *Mishnah* 15. Rabbi Yannai said. "It is not in our participation to either explain the prosperity of the wicked nor the tribulation of the righteous." Rabbi Mania ben Cheresh said. "Be first in the salutation of peace to all men and be rather a tail to the lions than a head to the foxes." How frequently we have heard that God does not allow anything bad to happen to the righteous. If anything bad happens. "The devil did it!" Sometimes I almost feel sorry for the devil. The devil gets blamed for almost everything, things he did not have one single thing to do with. However, we have to have a scapegoat.

I am skipping over to Chapter 5, *Mishnah* 23, to one little sentence, quoting Rabbi ben Hai Hai. He said. "According to the suffering is the reward." Hai Hai was a contemporary of Rabbi ben Bag Bag. We know very little about these men, just the one sentence quoted in *Mishnah* 22 and 23. They were probably contemporaries with Hillel, because in the *Avot d' Rabbi Natan* these sayings are ascribed to Hillel.

Ben Hai Hai said, "According to the suffering is the reward." That is just the opposite of what many have been told. Actually, this does not really mean what it might appear to on the surface. Ben Hai Hai was not trying to correct 20th century theology. What he said is pregnant with meaning. The more one labors in acquiring knowledge and the knowledge of God, the more one labors in practicing the commandments of law, the greater one's reward is going to be. Accumulation, or the acquiring of knowledge does not come without suffering. It is not easy. It is difficult. It only comes at a great cost – and you have to be willing to pay it. The greater price you pay, the more you will be able to do; thus, the greater your reward will be. Notice again the emphasis upon doing.

In *Mishnah* 22 of Chapter 4, Rabbi Elazar ha-Kapar used to say, "They that are born are destined to die, and the dead are destined to be brought to life again, and the living are destined after death to be judged, to know, to make known, and to understand that He is God. He is the Maker. He is the Creator. He is the discerner. He is the judge. He is the witness. He is the plaintiff, and he it is that shall judge the future. Blessed be he with whom there is no unrighteousness, nor forgetfulness, nor respecter of persons...and in the hereafter, you will have to give account and reckoning before the king of kings, the holy one, blessed be He."

Not only is this *Mishnah* very Pharasaic, it is also very Pauline which, of course, is to be expected in view of the fact that Paul refers to himself as "a Pharisee of the Pharisees." In *1 Corinthians* 15, what is the theme? The resurrection from the dead. "We are not all going to die, but some will be changed in a moment, in the twinkling of an eye, at the sound of the last trump, and we will be changed and this mortal will put on immortality, and we will all be caught up to be with the Lord in the air." This is the Jewish and very Pharisaic idea of life after death and of the reward of the righteous.

Here is an interesting *Mishnah* and, frankly, I do not know that there is a lot of commentary that is needed to accompany it. We will let the reading of it serve as its own commentary. "There are seven characteristics of an uncultured person and seven of a wise man. A wise man does not speak before one who is superior to him in wisdom; he does not break in upon the words of his fellow; he is not hasty to answer; he questions in accordance with the subject matter, and makes answer to the point; he speaks upon the first thing first, and upon the last thing last; and regarding what he has not heard, he says, 'I do not understand it'; and he admits the truth. And the reverse of all these is characteristic of an uncultured man."

In *Mishnah* 16 of Chapter 5, "If love depended on some material cause and the material cause passes away, so shall it pass: but if it does not depend upon some material cause, it will never pass away." Remember again the words of Paul in *1 Corinthians* 12. "Though I speak with the tongues of men and angels and have not love, I am become as sounding brass or a tinkling cymbal."

I want to emphasize again that the ideas reflected here in the *Chapters of the Fathers* can be found in the teachings of all of the *New Testament* writers which, again, is just what we should expect. Why? Because they are all Jews. They all came from the same background, the same religious and spiritual heritage.

*Mishnah* 19, Chapter 5 says, "Whoever has these three characteristics is of the disciples of Abraham our father, but he in whom there are three other attributes is of Balaam the wicked. A good eye, a lowly mind, and a humble soul are the traits of the disciples of Abraham our father. An evil eye, a haughty mind and a proud soul are the characteristics of the disciples of Balaam the wicked. And what is the difference between the disciples of our father Abraham and the disciples of the wicked Balaam? The disciples of our father Abraham enjoy this world, and inherit the world to come. But the disciples of the wicked Balaam inherit *Gehenna* and descend to the pit of destruction."

Notice that the first characteristic of the disciple of Abraham is the good eye, generosity, *tzedakah*, an ever recurring theme, the central or foundational theme of biblical faith. The next is the humble spirit, the broken or the wounded, or poor in spirit, the humble soul. Here we see a principal characteristic of Hebrew prose and poetry parallelisms, two statements that are parallel one to the other, that are structured in almost the same way as Jesus presents them in the *Beatitudes*. "Blessed are the poor in spirit...Blessed are the meek...Blessed are they that mourn." Who are they? They are all the same. To be poor in spirit is to be uncompromisingly righteous. To be uncompromisingly righteous is to yearn after God and the things of God.

Notice that the structure is almost identical to that of the *Beatitudes*. What are the three sayings? A good eye, or generosity, one who is lowly of spirit, and one who is humble of soul. And the opposite of these are the characteristics of the disciples of Balaam who, this *Mishnah* tells us, will inherit *Gehenna*. But the disciples of Abraham, what of them? Notice that they are to enjoy this world, the things of this world and, ultimately, inherit the world to come. Where do we hear something like that? "Blessed are the meek for they shall inherit the earth." (*Matthew* 5 and *Psalm* 37).

In *Mishnah* 20, Judah ben Tema said, "Be strong as the leopard and light as the eagle and fleet as the hart and mighty as the lion to do the will of thy father who is in heaven." Again, the emphasis is upon doing. Biblical faith is not a creed or belief in a certain statement of faith. Biblical faith has very little to do with what one says but, rather, what one does. Biblical faith is not so much man always directing his attention upward toward God but, rather, through acts of *tzedakah*, reaching out to others, meeting them at the point of their need and assisting in making them whole. This is the foundation of biblical faith, of what it means to be in the kingdom, a part of the kingdom, what it means to be kingdom. It is not withdrawing from the world and forming some kind of bless me club or praise-the-Lord society, but it is being busy in doing for others, acts of *tzedakah*, of *gemilut hasadim*, principles with which we began our study. Principles of biblical faith are not directed upward. It is not something one does for God. It is directed outward toward one's fellow man, but in so doing, at one and the same time, one performs the will of the Father.

# BIBLIOGRAPHY

Blackman, Phillip, *The Mishnah*, Judaica Press, New York, 2000.

Cohen, Abraham, *Every Man's Talmud: The Major Teachings of the Rabbinic Sages*, Schocken, New York, 1995.

Flusser, David, (Prof), *Jewish Sources in Early Christianity*, Mod Books, New York, 1989.

Goldin, Judah, (Translator), *The Fathers According to Rabbi Nathan*, Yale University Press, New Haven, 1990.

Young, Brad, *Jewish Background to the Lord's Prayer*, Gospel Research Foundation, 1984.

# ABOUT THE AUTHOR

 Dr. Roy B. Blizzard is President of Bible Scholars, Inc., an Austin-based corporation dedicated to biblical research and education. A native of Joplin, Missouri, he attended Oklahoma Military Academy and has a B.A. degree from Phillips University in Enid, Oklahoma. He has an M.A. degree from Eastern New Mexico University in Portales, New Mexico, an M.A. degree from the University of Texas at Austin, and a Ph.D. in Hebrew Studies from the University of Texas at Austin. From 1968 to June 1974, he was an instructor in Hebrew, Biblical History and Biblical Archaeology at the University of Texas at Austin. Dr. Blizzard is today a professor at the American Institute for Advanced Biblical Studies in Little Rock, Arkansas.

Dr. Blizzard has spent much of his time in Israel and the Middle East in study and research. He has hosted over 500 television programs about Israel and Judaism for various television networks and is a frequent television and radio guest. He is the author of numerous books and articles which can be found listed on the Bible Scholars Website, in the bookstore.

Dr. Blizzard is nationally certified as an educator in Marriage and Family relationships and human sexuality. He is a Diplomate with the American Board of Sexology and continues to conduct a private practice in the field of sex education and therapy.

OTHER BOOKS BY ROY B. BLIZZARD

*The Bible Sex and You*

*Tithing Giving and Prosperity*

*The Mountain of the Lord*

*Let Judah Go Up First: A Study in Praise, Prayer, and Worship*

David Bivin and Roy Blizzard, Jr., *Understanding the Difficult Words of Jesus: New Insights From a Hebrew Perspective*

Bible Scholars, Inc.
P. O. Box 204073
Austin, Texas 78720

www.biblescholars.org

*Dedicated to supporting, developing and promoting future Bible Scholars.*

Printed in Poland
by Amazon Fulfillment
Poland Sp. z o.o., Wrocław